P9-CMQ-391

THILL Publication - Brussels

Uitgeverij THILL N.V. Brussel · Tel. 344.92.40
Fotografisch materiaal: THILL
Lay-out: J.J. DE MOL
Gedrukt in EEG, Litovald

D/1983/3217/6

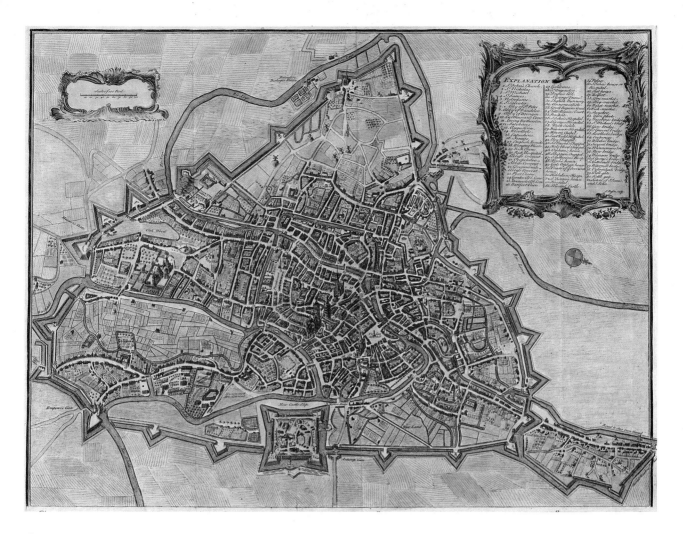

Ghent was founded in the seventh century around the two abbeys of Saint Baaf and Saint Peter. At that time the town was known as Ganda. Today the old town lies between the rivers Schelde and Leie and consists of small, narrow streets. Around the eleventh century the town was destroyed by the Normans. As a result the counts of Flanders decided to build a fortified stronghold, which later became known as the Gravensteen. Around this stronghold there grew up a centre of trade. In this manner Ghent became the capital of Flanders. The lace and linen trade experienced an enormous growth. Large oceangoing ships brought to the town the glory and riches of distant lands. Industrious Ghent with its independent, stubborn and hard-working inhabitants became a city of world importance during the Middle Ages. In the fourteenth century the city was wracked by civil conflicts. The wealthy lace trader, Jacob Van Artevelde, was killed by the rioters. The inhabitants wanted a share in the city's government, and the well organized guilds joined in this political struggle. The counts attempted to retain power in their own hands and this led to clashes. The House of Burgundy became the new opponent of the strife-ridden city. The fifteenth century was marked by a struggle for power. In 1492, the city was forced to sign the Peace Treaty of Cadzand whereby limits were placed on its independence. This independence finally came to an end in 1540. In the seventeenth century the city was the scene of sieges and war. Only in the eighteenth century did it experience a return to economic prosperity through the establishment of new industries.

The University was founded in Ghent during the reign of William I, and the canal linking the city to Terneuzen was completed in 1827. This canal enabled Ghent to become a sea port and this was a key factor in its economic development.

Ghent lies in the middle of garden nurseries and is proud of its world-famous "Ghent flower show".

The Cathedral of Saint Baaf has its origin in a chapel founded in 942 and dedicated to Saint John the Baptist, the oldest patron saint of the trading city. In 1274, the wealthy lace traders of the Middle Ages built a church over this chapel which is a masterpiece of Gothic architecture. In 1462, the first stone was laid of the towers that were completed in 1569. The emperor Charles was baptised in this still incompleted church. In 1550, he granted it a sum of money in order to provide the church with arched windows filled with stained glass.

The present-day high altar, made of marble, gilded wood, copper and bronze, dates from the beginning of the eighteenth century. In the chancel stands the sepulchral monument of Antoon Triest, one of the major benefactors of the cathedral, and Bishop of Ghent from 1621 to 1657.
The sculpture of white and black marble is the work of Jeroom Duquesnoy. The most interesting piece of church furniture is the pulpit. The rococco art found therein is the work of Laurent Delvaux and the pulpit was completed in 1745.

The cathedral is a powerful monument of gothic architecture. It is a museum of sculpture, carving, wrought iron work and painting.
The most famous painting, "the Adoration of the Lamb of God", is housed in a chapel specially built for this purpose. This masterpiece is commonly attributed to the two brothers, Jan and Hubert Van Eyck.

From the square of the Cathedral of Saint Baaf, there is a general view of the Belfort and the Hall towers.

In this square can be seen the statue of the man of letters, Jan Frans Willems (1793-1846), which was made by the artist, Isidoor Derudder.

The Royal Flanders Arts House was designed in the Flemish Renaissance style and is the work of the architect, Edward De Vigne. The mosaic roof scene was painted by C. Montald. It is a mythological scene depicting "Apollo and the Muses of Parnassus". This work is an ode to the performing arts and was completed in 1898.

At the foot of the powerful Belfort stretches the Lace Hall, which was built between 1425 and 1445 according to the plans of Simon Van Assche. This once served as the meeting place of the powerful merchants of the cloth industry who made the city prosperous in the Middle Ages.

The municipal prison, adjacent to the Hall towers, has a facade dating from 1741 with a demi-relief that presents the Ancient Roman, Cimon. Cimon was sentenced to death by starvation and was nursed by his daughter. Hence the popular name of "De Mammelokker" (the allurer of maidens) that was given to this building.

9

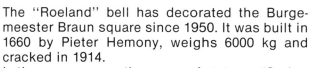

The "Roeland" bell has decorated the Burge-meester Braun square since 1950. It was built in 1660 by Pieter Hemony, weighs 6000 kg and cracked in 1914.
In the same square the group of statues, "Spring of the Bereaved", by the Ghent sculptor, George Minne, can be seen.

The Belfort was built in the thirteenth and fourteenth centuries. Jan Van Haelst and Filips van Beergine built the Belfort with stone from Doornik and worked together with the joiner, Jan Broncard. The city of Ghent needed a special building wherein it could keep the charters granting it its privileges, and from where the city guard called be called out. In "Het Secreet", the lowest room in the Belfort, the precious charters and documents granting privileges were kept.

The room had two doors each fitted with three locks, with the keys being in the hands of different craft guilds.

The documents were kept in a chest with eighteen draws and which was in turn locked by three keys; of these keys, one was kept by the bailiff and the two others by the city wardens.

The guards on the towers had to tour the battlements on the hour in order to demonstrate that they were not asleep. Their tasks included keeping a look-out for a possible enemy, to raise the alarm in the event of fire, and to ring the bells during times of great danger.

The Beiaard, consisting of 44 bells, is one of the best known carillons in the Low Countries.

The present-day spire was only completed in 1913 and is the work of the master-builder Valentin Vaerewijck.

The enormous copper dragon, built in Ghent in 1377, managed to survive all the changes brought by the centuries. This fabulous beast has been for centuries the symbolic guardian of the city's freedoms. There are several popular legends doing the rounds but the question of when it breathed fire for the first time remains in dispute.

The first Church of Saint Nicholas was built around the middle of the eleventh century; it was, however, destroyed by two fires, in 1120 and 1176. The growth in trade and industry made it possible for the citizens to rebuild the church. The chancel and the nave were completed between 1220 and 1250. The towers were designed entirely in the Schelde-gothic style.

In the thirteenth century the chancel was extended by means of a number of outer chapels that were each erected by a different trade guild. Around the fourteenth century the entire structure became liable to collapse; stones were put into position in order to strengthen the entire structure but this led to loss of the church's high, bright and symetrical aspect. Until the Belfort was built, the towers were used as a guard post for the defence of the city.

The church's treasures were destroyed by ransackers.

During the French Revolution, the church was used as a horse stable.

In its facades the town hall bears the traces of six centuries of construction history. On the right one can see the De Keure late gothic magistrates' house with its excess of light ornamentation; on the left one can see the Van Gedele magistrates' house with its more sober renaissance style.

One of the most delightful parts of the late gothic section is the staircase which was designed by the Brabant architects, Rombout Keldermans and Dominicis de Waeghemaekere at the time of the Emperor Charles (1518).

It was under the Emperor Charles that the Pacification Room was built as well; it was here that the De Keure magistrates held their hearings. The famous labyrinth floor reminds the visitors of this. Pacification was a peace treaty that was concluded in the town hall in 1576 between the Protestants and Catholics.

The Arsenal Room of 1482 served as the meeting place of the notorious Ghent Collatie or people's council that repeatedly instigated the revolts against the aristocracy. Later it was used as the weapons room of the town guard.

The impressive chimney and the painted arched roof are original.

The Cabinet of the Mayor of 1728 is completely intact Louis XIV interior. Above all, the stucco ceiling and the marble chimney testify to the artistry and the skill of our ancestors.

The Throne Room contains the coronation throne of Joseph II and various large paintings that once decorated the town during the colourful entry parades of the aristocrats.

The present-day reception salon was once the members chamber of the States of Flanders and recalls the Spanish and Austrian administrations, particulary by its baroque chimney and stucco ceiling, and by the portraits of the Habsburg dynasty.

The sober office was part of the treasury or town finance house offices. The painting on the ceiling is by Jan van Cleef (1696); the paintings above the fireplace and the wall panelling are by Pieter van Reysschoot (around 1770).

Portrait of Empress Maria Theresa in the reception salon. The dress of Flemish lace that the Empress is wearing was a gift to her from the states of Flanders. The dress was made by Ghent orphans. Out of gratitude for this expensive present, Marie Theresa, allowed her portrait to be painted by her court painter, Martin von Meytens, after which the completed work was handed over to the members of the states.

Since the early Middle Ages, the Cornmarket has been the commercial and economical centre of the city. Various historical buildings with interesting facades can be seen there.

The neo-gothic Post Office (1910) is the work of Stephane Mortier and Louis Cloquet. It is a mixture of the gothic and renaissance styles. Its luxurious decorations represent, as it were, a historical panorama in stone.

The Graslei was the busy port area full of traders, dock workes, porters, bakers and brouwers who came here to offer their wares. The interesting buildings are still one of the glories of the city. Their reflections can be glimpsed in the Leie river and give a living impression of the wealth and the power of the guilds.

— Guild hall of the bricklayers, Brabant gothic (1527).
— The first corn measurers house, Flemish renaissance (1435).
— The Warehouse in the oldest building in the Graslei, twelth to thirteenth centuries.

The city of Ghent has the right to claim a quarter of all the grain being transported along the Schelde or the Leie rivers. This was then stored for a week or two and sold at a later date.

— The toll house (1682) in the Flemish renaissance style is wedged between two large guild halls.
— Guild hall of the grain measurers (1698) in the late baroque style.
— Guild hall of the independent shippers in the Brabant gothic style (1531) by the Ghent architect Christoffel Van den Berghe. This is one of the most attractive buildings. Above the door can be seen the bas-relief of a ship that was used for the Baltic voyage.

The vegetable market was always the place for the sale of fish. Since the eighteenth century there has been a vegetable market held there every day, except Sundays; on that day it makes way for the art market.
On the "Galgenhuisje" can still be seen iron clamps that were used for the Medieval pillory.
The Empire pump is the work of the architect P.J. De Broe.

The building used for the Meat Hall, designed by Gillis de Suttere, was begun in 1407 and completed in 1419. The main facade and the extensive side facades, that are reflected in thewater are interesting examples of the architecture of the Ghent merchant class. The chapel that was attached to it was later integrated into the Hall itself. The windows can be seen from the river.

Together with the Graslei, the Koornlei was the centre of the Medieval port. From the beginning of this century onwards, the splendid house were restored according to their original plans which had been preserved.

The house called "De Lintworm" is particularly interesting; it was built originally of Roman stone, around 1200.

This was the house belonging to Egmont, the hero who resisted the Spanish regime. He is the main character in the Egmont Overture by Beethoven.

The Guild Hall of the non-indipendent shippers with its baroque facade (1739) is known under the name "Het Anker" and has a sailing ship as a weathercock.

In the stately aristocratic house of Ridder de Coninck a Museum of Ornamental Art has been established. It contains the most tasteful furniture that once filled the homes of the Ghent governing class of the eighteenth century. It also contains examples of the art of cloth production and of present-day artistic production.

"Huis der Gekroonde Hoofden" with a renaissance facade dating from 1559 that shows the sculpted faces of the Counts of Flanders, from Baldwin of Constantinople to Philip II.

The Castle of the Counts (Gravenkasteel) was originally a stronghold that was built by Count Baldwin I around the year 868.

It was rebuilt on the instructions of Philip van der Elzas, Count of Flanders. The sign above the gateway shows the date 1180. Above the entrance there is an opening in the shape of a cross which refers to the Count's participation in the Crusades from 1177 to 1178. He died in the Holy Land during the siege of Akko.

The Gravensteen was the seat of the aristocratic court of the Council of Flanders. Innumerable rooms and cellars were used as a prison. The impressive feudal castle has survived the centuries. Inside the counts' private quarters a museum of torture appliances has been established. From the top of the castle tower there is an incomparable view of the surroundings. The historical heart of the city can be admired as well as the residential and industrial areas beyond.

Saint Veerler square. The harmonious series of house facades that extend around the square date from the sixteenth century. Only the entrance to the Oude Vismijn (seventeenth century) is an exception to this rule. Over the monumental entrance in the baroque style is a statue of Neptune with his trident and of the Divinities of the two rivers of Ghent, the Leie and the Schelde.

On the corner of the Kraanlei stands the "De Fluitspeler" house in the baroque style which has a richly decorated upper facade dating from 1669.
Next to it can be seen the "Zeven Werken van Barmhartigheid" house that looks toward the Alijn hospital where the matchless Museum of Medicine is housed.

Further on along the street, in one of the historical facades, is the Ghent version of the Manneken Pis which, according to specialists, is much older than its brother in Brussels but less well known. This too is pure folklore.

The Museum of Folklore has been housed since 1962 in the building used by the Alijn childrens' hospital that was completely restored according to the plans drawn up by Valentin Vaerewijck. The alms house or hospice was inhabited by 18 poor women until the middle of the nineteenth century. On 8 November 1883, it was sold and thereafter served as a residence for the families of workers. The municipal administration of Ghent revoked this charter in 1941, and later made the building available for housing the Museum of Folklore.

The Museum is Mainly devoted to social life in Ghent at the turn of the century with its different trades and activities.

In the puppet theatre there are regular puppet shows featuring the traditional Ghent puppet, "Pierke".

Old tavern, ca 1900, with bar, glass rack, cafe organ by A. Corsini, cafe games; vestiges of club games: teerlingbak, vogelpik...

Fully fitted-out chemist's shop with a collection of chemist's articles dating from the seventeenth to the nineteenth centuries.

Candle mould dating from the second half of the nineteenth century. Moulder and extinguishing bucket in earthenware dating from the seventeenth century.

The pipe and tobacco collection has a very large selection of pipes, snuff, tobacco pouches and tobacco cutting tools.

The bathroom has one of the first metallic bathtubs and gas water-heaters dating from the second half of the nineteenth century as well as a washing seat and a linen press.

Bread and cake shop. Various bakery products including hard wood rollers, Ghent pouts and pepper bowls; a fine collection of baking moulds.

Prebend's living quarters. Interior of a poor person who was allowed to live in the Alijn hospice.

The "Dulle Griet" is a cast iron cannon that was built at some stage between 1430 and 1481. It has a lenght of 5 metres and weighs 1600 kg.

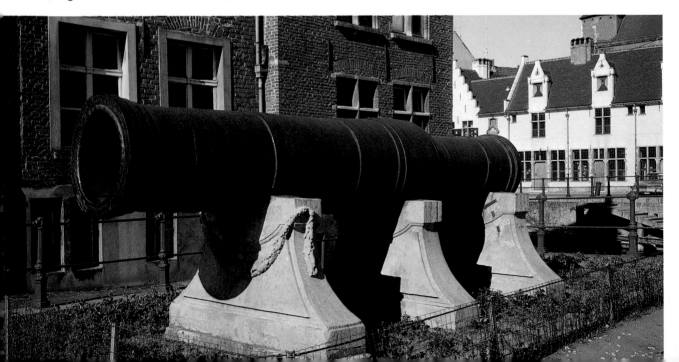

The "Toreken" is the guild hall of the curriers. The building dates from 1483 has a stone tower and a typical stepped gabel. The "Maria" bell is housed in this tower and is rung at the opening of the markets. The first Church of Saint James was built in 1093 and was dedicated to the patron saint of the seafarers whose protection was requested against hunger. It was destroyed by fire in 1120 but was immediately rebuilt. Practically every part of the church has been changed throughout the ages. Only the central tower has remained intact. The two western towers remind us of churches in Normandy. In the nineteenth century it was restored in the neogothic style which makes it almost impossible to recognize the original outline of the construction.

The Friday Market was the forum of Ghent. Innumerable festivities, quarrels and fights took place there in succession. The fate of the market was tiep up with that of the guilds and their activities. During the Middle Ages the weavers and spinners were most in evidence there and they were most inclined to quarrel. Ghent was first and foremost a wool town and as long as the wool trade went well, the town prospered. The friendship of Jacob Van Artevelde and Edward III was of great significance to Ghent but also for other Flemish towns. The negotiations between the two did not also lead to the most desirable result. The last piece of news that he came back home with did not always meet with the approval of his fellow citizens. In 1345, Van Artevelde was murdered by rioters. The artist, P. Devigne, painted the town governor in an aristocratic and energetic pose, in the manner in which he always addressed his people.

The Church of Saint Stephen was build in 1606 and was repeatedly rebuilt. Following a fire in 1838, it was restored. The church entrance, with its door artistically decorated with a carving in oak, dates from the seventeenth century. There are altar paintings by Gaspar De Craeyer.

The Monastery of Saint Augustine was built at the end of the thirteenth century by Gerelmus Borluut. He was the son of this rich family of the governing class that studied in Paris and came into contact with the Augustinians. He gave the order a piece of land on which they built extensively and where they carried out teaching activities. At the time of the Reformation the monastery was destroyed and two of the monks were burned alive. On the order of the King of Spain, Ghent had to rebuild the monestery. The church was consecrated in 1615. In 1838, the buildings were destroyed by fire but were rebuilt in the form in which they are found today. The old infirmery gives a view on to the Saint Augustine wharf.

The Donkere Poort is a vestige of the Court of the Princes (Prinsenhof) where, on 24 February 1500, the Emperor Charles, the oldest son of Philip the Handsome and Joan of Castille, saw the light of day. At that time no-one yet knew that this scion would one day rule over the Low Countries, Spain and the Holy Roman Empire. The Archduke Albrecht and his lady, Isabella, were the last aristocrats to live in the Prinsenhof. It was pulled down in the eighteenth century.

The Rabot is an example of the strenghtened city gates.
It was built in 1486 during a difficult period that followed the death of Maria of Burgundy in 1482. This door was so strong that repeated attempts by the Emperor Frederick III to conquer the city with 40,000 soldiers along this route were in vain.

The Oude Begijnhof was founded in 1242 thanks to the bounty of Joan of Constantinople. Up to the beginning of the fifteenth century its inhabitants lived a very frugal life therein. Some of the later houses with stepped gabels, front gardens and baroque entrances have been preserved and still stand around the church.

The Church of Holy Elizabeth, built in 1638, is one of the oldest beguinage churches in the Low Countries. Its two tall towerlets with rounded spires give it a special architectural character.

The Abbey of the Unshod Carmelites was founded in the seventeenth century, and the abbey buildings have a sombre aspect. The church was built between 1703 and 1712 in a strongly classical style. The interior of the eighteenth century is very homogenous with an inner doorway in marble and oak, three baroque altars, and tasteful pulpit and confessionals.

The Church of Saint Michael was begun in 1440 and completed in 1648. At the time of the Burgundian Dukes the note of architectural ostentation was increased. It is a spacious church in the late gothic style. The massive tower remains unfinished.

From the Saint Michael bridge there is an attractive view in all directions. On the one side, the guild halls of the Graslei and the fortified towers of the Gravensteen and, on the other side, the stately Church of Saint Michael and, further afield, the famous row of the towers of Ghent with, in the centre and perched high on its spire, the golden dragon of the Belfort.

The first stone of the "Grote Aula" was laid in 1819. The pompous entrance of the university was finished in 1826. Louis Roelandt was the architect of this neo-classical work that reminds one of the Pantheon in Rome. King William I of Orange, a benefactor of the city, wished to see the latter make strides in the intellectual field as well. After a number of intrigues, the King chose Ghent as the site of the university he wished to establish. As early as 1819 the first students were studying for their degrees. The town was very proud of its university and decided to build this palace to house it.

Hotel Van der Haeghen is a wealthy governor's house from the eighteenth century. It was here that the French-speaking playwright and poet of Ghent, Maurice Maeterlinck, had his office. Maeterlinck was born in Ghent in 1862 and died in Nice in 1949. The office contains objects, documents and a collection of letters by this Nobel Prize winner.

In this office that also bears his name can also be seen the graphic work by the Ghent artist Victor Stuyvaert.

The "Kouter" was the meeting place of the city's inhabitants. It was here that festivities were organized and meetings of the townspeople held.

The guild of Saint Sebastian held its archery contests here as welle between the sixteenth and eighteenth centuries. The splendid aristocratic house, the "Faligan", that was built on the instructions of Hector Faligan in 1755 in imitation of the fifteenth century style, also stands in the Kouter.

The Royal Opera House dates from between 1837 and 1940.

The statue of Jan Palfijn (1650-1730) stands in the public park. It is the work of Godfried de Vreeze. This famous Flemish doctor was the discoverer of forceps and the founder of anatomy. He achieved and international repute.

The Court of Justice (1836-1846) is a very imposing building which stands majestically along two watercourses. With its colums, and its windows with their triangular frontons that are repeated in the main theme of the entrance, it presents a harmonious whole. It is the work of the architect Louis Roelandt.

The Cistercian abbey of Bijloke was founded in the thirteenth century. A hospital was attached to this abbey and this later became the Municipal Hospital of the city of Ghent.

The buildings were constructed at different periods. The refectory, the dormitory and the cloisters date from the fourteenth century. The so-called "House of the Abbess" was built at the beginning of the seventeenth century. The Museum of Antiquity of the city of Ghent was established in the period 1925-1928 in the buildings of the old Bijloke abbey. At that time the entrance door of the former Groot Begijnhof of Saint Elisabeth of Ghent, that dates from 1660, was moved to this site.

Fireplace of the Treasury. This multi-coloured fireplace of the seventeenth century, designed by Norbert Sauvage and decorated with a painting by Jan van Cleef, was part of the old Treasury of the town hall and was rebuilt in the museum.

The meeting room of the Ghent guilds. The reconstructed meeting room of the Ghent civil guard guilds (Saint Joris, Saint Sebastian, Saint Antony and Saint Michael) offers. On account of its numerous objects, a living picture of its past. Not only registers, documents, paintings, but also jewels and objects of value of these guilds have been preserved inside.

During processions and ceremonies the guild members carried their emblems, banners and had their torch holders. The painted wooden torch holders of the seventeenth and eighteenth centuries are crowned with a design that conveys the guild, its trade or its patron saints.

The examples dipicted belonged to the twiners, the ship makers, the stone workers and the masons.

The Dormitory. In the fourteenth century dormitory, that originally occupied the entire upper floor of the east wing of the abbey, there are mementoes of the trades of Ghent. These include the miniature of a warship of the seventeenth century that was later carried by the Independent Shippers guild in the Ommegang procession of Saint Macharius. Silver, copper and bronze objects bear witness to the enterprising qualities of the trade guilds.

The Bijloke Museum contains precious examples of old municipal institutions. The gilded and silver emblems of the Ghent town-beadles are exceptional examples of this. These examples were designed by the gold and silversmith, Cornelius De Bont.

Almost all of the artistic activities of the guilds are represented in this museum. Particularly noteworthy among the earthenware of the Middle Ages, mainly found inGhent and the surrounding area, are the statuettes of riders of the thirteenth and fourteenth centuries.

Coat of armour of a herald. This splendid coat of armour of the sixteenth century, bordered with a multi-coloured fringe, was worn by the herald during the coronation of the Spanish kings as counts of Flanders.

The most varied and important collection in the museum also includes a selection of Medieval weapons, with examples of the so-called "goedendag", the much feared axe and pike weapon.

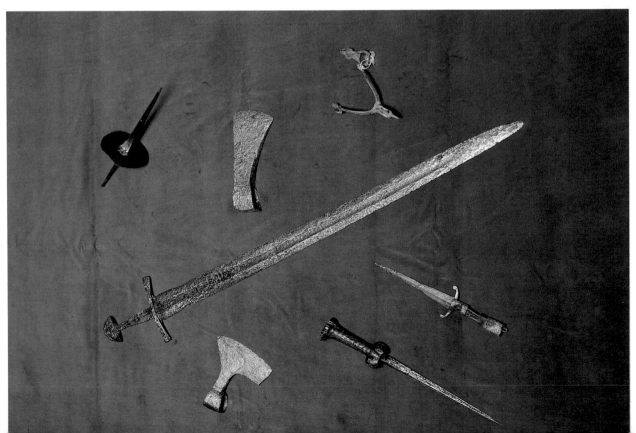

Stylish seventeenth century interiors with open hearth, wooden ceiling, furniture and paintings, mostly coming from former Ghent abbeys and alms houses, were to be found in the "House of the Abbess". The kitchen with the associated household effects and the sitting-room depicted here belong to the ensemble.

A splendid example of the fourteenth century brick architecture is the west facade of the refectory that is justifiably recognized as an architectural masterpiece.
The so-called "House of the Abbess", built in the years 1613 to 1616, once served as the infirmary of the nuns.

The Belle Epoque statue of Charles de Kerckhove de Denterghem (1819-1882) was made by Hippoliet Leroy. He was the mayor of the city from 1857 to 1881 and has several modernization projects to his credit.

The statue of Oswald de Kerckhove de Denterghem (1844-1906) stands in the middle of the pergola of the park. It was made by the Ghent artist Gustaaf Van den Meersche. He was an outstanding court architect and scholar.

Emiel Claus (1849-1924) was the defender and the flag-bearer of impressionism in Flanders. The statue is by Yvonne Serruys based on a design by Oscar Van der Voorde.

The Municipal Palace of Festivities (Stedelijk Feestpaleis) (1913) is an architectural complex wherein the internationally renowned five-yearly flower show is held. It is a pleasure to gaze at all these beautiful flowers and plants.

The Museum of Fine Art of Ghent can be found in the Citadel park. It was built according to the plans of Charles Van Rijsselberghe. The official opening took place in 1904.
The art collection contains paintings, sculptures, drawings and graphics from the fourteenth to the twentieth century.
There are many temporary exhibitions which are held there from time to time and which enjoy a high reputation.

The ceremonies room of the museum is decorated with two series of tapestries which come from the Gravensteen and the Abbey of Saint Peter. Both series were woven in workshops in Brussels and originate respectively in the seventeenth and eighteenth centuries.

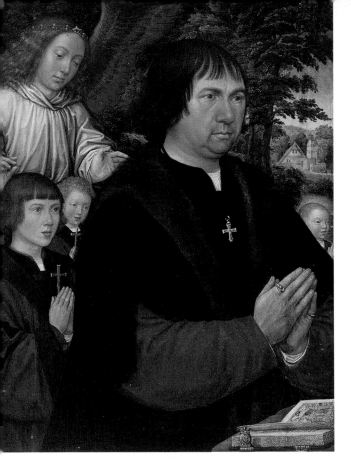

These portraits are attributed to a Ghent master working at the beginning of the sixteenth century. They were originally the two side panels of a triptych.

View of an exhibition room in the museum. Inside can be found, in addition to the oil paintings by Rubens, paintings by van Jordaens, Van Dijck, Cornelis De Vos and Gaspard De Crayer.

"The temptation of H. Hieronymus" is, like "The Cross-Bearer", a masterpiece of Hieronymus Bosch. Both works are among the most celebrated belonging to the Old Masters section of the Museum of Fine Art. The great personality of the artist, who lived and worked in 's Hertogenbosch, shines from the work that has still not been completely demystified.

This "Study of the head of a young moor" by Gaspard De Crayer reminds one of the negro heads painted by P.P. Rubens. In the same way as many other artists, this painter from Antwerp, born in 1584, came under the influence of Rubens and retained this style all his life.

This "Portrait of a kleptomaniac" was painted by Theodore Gericault on the instruction of a Parisian doctor who made a study of madness. It is an undisputed masterpiece of this artist who died in 1824 aged only thirty three.

Camille Corot who painted this exceptionally fine work "Stonequarry by Fontainebleau" is one of the harbingers of the Barbizon school. This group of artists that worked in the forest of Fontainebleau is represented in the museum collection by a few fine works by Daubigny.

James Ensor is the most important and the most innovative artist from the Belgian school towards the end of the nineteenth century. The fame that he enjoys extends beyond our borders. The painting "Old lady with masks" dates from 1889 and is held to be one of his major works.

It goes without saying that the Museum of Fine Art in Ghent devotes a special place to the work of the Flemish impressionists. They are all represented there: Servaes, Permeke, Frits Van den Berghe and Gust De Smet.
This "Village Feast" illustrates in a fine manner the extent to which the artist made this style into a personal one.

"Balkon van Manet"
MAGRITTE 1950.

"Verlust der mitte"
ASGER JORN 1958.

"Piewan" 1975
Deltavliegtuig P I"
"U-controle III" 1972.
PANAMARENKO

Herinnering aan de dood
van mijn moeder"
ROGER RAVEL 1965.

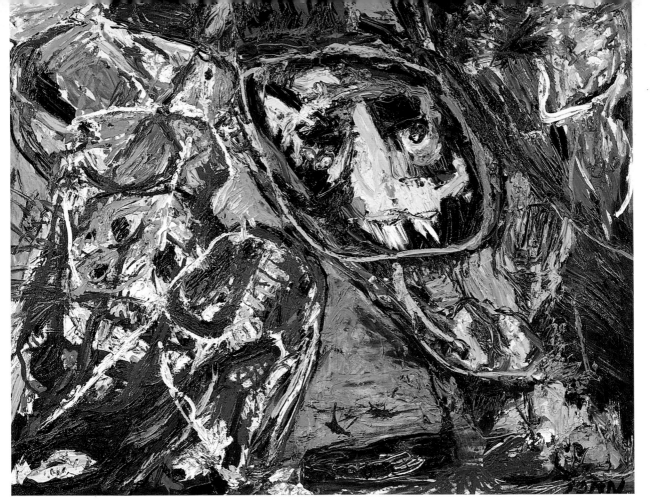

The Abbey of Saint Peter was founded at the end of the seventh century by a friend of the Holy Amandus. Several quarrels arose between the monks of Saint Baafs and the nuns of Saint Peters. They displayed an unbecoming zeal in their desire to acquire relics. The Abbey Church of Saint Peters was destroyed during the troubles of 1570-1580. At the end of the sixteenth century the southern part of the Low Countries came under the rule of Isabella, daughter of Philip I of Spain, and her husband, Albrecht. An end was put to these religious quarrels. The new rulers were Roman Catholics. Several churches were restored or rebuilt that had suffered during these quarrels. The Archduke Albrecht and Isabella gave instructions to P. Huyssens to restore the Abbey Church. The latter rebuilt the old gothic church in the baroque style with a dome in imitation of the Church of Saint Ignatius in Rome. The present-day abbey premises were built during 1592 and 1634. Today exhibitions and cultural events are regularly held there.

Most of the houses of the Kleine Begijnhof date from the seventeenth and eighteenth centuries. Nonetheless the layout of the Klein Begijnhof is roughly consistent with that of the Medieval begijnhof.

The construction of the present-day church was begun in 1658. The facade with its monumental entrance was built totally out of natural stone and is a splendid example of the Flemish baroque. It has a very harmonious and bright interior.

This peaceful and motionless corner of Ghent was one the wealthy Begijnhof.

The Abbey of Saint Baaf owes its name to the rich convert who was the benefactor of the abbey which was founded in the seventh century by the Holy Amandus.

The first stone of the church was laid in 985 by Abt Odwin but only in 1067 was a portion of this holy ground consecrated. The abbey was destroyed by the Vikings.

Important changes were made in the fifteenth century. In 1540, the Emperor Charles decided that he needed a new fortress in order to keep the city firmly under control. As a result, a large portion of the abbey was pulled down. The lavatorium, the refectory, a part of the chapter-room, the brewery, the dormitory and the large church, all dating from the twelth century, today make up the Museum of Stone Objects.

The statue of the Emperor Charles is a bronze copy of the original work that can be found in the Madrid Prado. It is the work of the Italian sculptor, Leone Leoni (1509-1590), who was attached to the imperial court.

The "De Kleine Sikkel" house is a roman-style governor's house dating from the thirteenth century. Above the earlier entrance the coat of arms of the Van der Sickelen family can still be seen.

In the Bauwenssquare stands the statue of Lieven Bauwens (1769-1822). He was the importer of mechanical spinning machines on to the continent and the promotor of the industrial development of Ghent.

"Geraard de Duivelsteen" is one of the largest and most delightful crypts of Ghent of olden times. It was built in 1245 by Ser Geeraard, nicknamed the Devil. He belonged to the master-builders who called themselves with pride "The Lords of Ghent". His own house looks on to the waterfront and it contains a number of high arrow-slits and four corner towers. Over the centuries it has been used for a variety of purposes.

The monument to the Van Eyck brothers can be found near a side entrance to the Cathedral of Saint Baaf. It was designed by the sculptor, Geo Verbanck; Valentijn Vaerwijck was responsible for the architectural execution. The unveiling took place on 9 August 1913 in the presence of King Albert of Belgium. This monument shows the artists Jan and Hubert Van Eyck receiving the hommage of the inhabitants.

"Hotel Vander Meersch" is currently a monastery. It has a wing dating from 1547 and was extended in the seventeenth century at the expense of J.B. Vander Meersche. The interior garden is decorated with rococo gabels. The interior is very richlt decorated.

The "Sint Jorishof" was the hall of the crossbow guild. The guild took to meeting there from 1381 onwards. The present-day building dates from the fifteenth century. In 1474, Maria of Burgundy laid the first stone of the guild hall chapel.

The "Achter Sikkel" lies in an exceptionally picturesque part of the city. This governor's house dating from the fourteenth century has been completely restored. It contains a number of galeries, towers and a house chapel with a small peaceful garden.

At the Hoogpoort can be found the "Serlippens" house, a majestic rococo house dating from the eighteenth century with a cast iron balcony.